D0923740

how to put on a

FASHION *show*

how to put on a

FASHION *show*

—

BY ERIC MUSGRAVE

BATSFORD

First published in the United Kingdom in 2014 by
Batsford
1 Gower Street
London WC1E 6HD
An imprint of Pavilion Books Group

Copyright © Batsford, 2014
Text © Eric Musgrave, 2014

The moral rights of the author have been asserted.

All rights reserved. No part of this publication may be reproduced,
stored in a retrieval system, or transmitted in any form or by any means,
electronic, mechanical, photocopying, recording or otherwise, without the
prior written permission of the copyright owner.

ISBN: 9781849941631

A CIP catalogue record for this book is available from the British Library.

10 9 8 7 6 5 4 3 2 1

Reproduction by Rival Colour Ltd, UK
Printed by 1010 Printing International Ltd, China

This book can be ordered direct from the publisher at the website:
www.pavilionbooks.com, or try your local bookshop.

PAGE 2 — The finale of the SS 2013 show by David Koma, a London-
based Georgian fashion designer.

OPPOSITE — Different-looking models, different outfits, but a common
hairstyle for the models at the AW14 show for Edeline Lee, a Korean-
Canadian designer working in London.

CONTENTS

INTRODUCTION

The fashion show is an essential element of the fashion industry. To present clothes on real-life moving models is to give them a three-dimensional existence that cannot be matched by images in a glossy magazine or garments hanging on a shop rail. Even a static presentation, at which the clothes are shown on mannequins or body forms, allows them to be seen on a human shape.

Fashion shows as we understand them today can trace their origins to the promotional presentations organized by American department store owners at the turn of the 20th century, although clothes makers had been giving private shows to selected customers as far back as the early 1800s. Today, the catwalk industry is a worldwide phenomenon with the four big biannual 'fashion weeks' in New York, London, Milan and Paris augmented by hundreds of smaller events around the world that use some sort of runway presentation as a platform from which to show, promote and sell fashion.

Over the last one-hundred-plus years the fashion show has advanced from restrained beginnings to theatrical extravaganzas. The polite private viewings in couture houses, at which 'fit models' (women on whom the designers fitted their prototype garments) showed the newest creations to select customers, proved that fashion shows were cost effective in terms of sales.

The early shows developed in the early 20th century were restrained and elegant, with gloved models carrying numbered cards to indicate which style they were wearing. Like so much else in fashion, the catwalk presentations changed significantly in the 1960s when designers sought to generate excitement for their new ready-to-wear collections. Loud music was introduced, the way the models walked became provocative and sexy, state-of-the-art lighting systems added drama, and elaborate stage sets and influences – from the whimsical to the shocking – were combined to generate publicity and sell a story.

What were once intimate and private gatherings for important clients, significant industry buyers or influential fashion journalists have now become global phenomena, streamed for free in real time on the internet, bringing the spectacle of the major designers' catwalks to a global audience.

This book sets out to assist those who wish to stage a fashion show. Whether a profile-raising exercise, part of a selling campaign, a social occasion, a charity event or just a celebratory party, the fashion show can take many forms. The options are limited only by budget and the imagination of the organizers. We cannot cover every possibility, but we hope that the guidelines outlined here will form a framework within which a memorable, enjoyable and exciting event can be created.

Eric Musgrave, London, 2014

RIGHT — A model strikes a pose backstage.

WHY STAGE A FASHION SHOW?

To successfully organize a fashion show you have to be clear about why you want to stage such an event. Does it have a tangible aim, such as wanting to sell the clothes you are presenting, or does it have an indirect aim, such as promoting your name or your company's name, or has it an aim for a third-party, such as raising money for a charity through a collection at the occasion? The question is: is this a business venture or a social venture? A fashion event can be staged for more than one reason but it is important to be clear about its aim if you are to execute it most effectively.

1. Most fashion shows are staged to present clothes (and related accessories) so that people will buy them. Those people may be professional buyers from stores and online retailers who will put down significant orders, or they might be the general public who will buy just individual pieces. In either case, or any other option, it is important that the clothes can be seen clearly and concisely. The merchandise should not be swamped or lost within a lavish production.

2. Conversely, some fashion shows are simply a spectacle, an entertainment, an experience. There is no great 'follow on' in these cases. They just remain in the memory as a fun and stimulating event, akin to going to the theatre or a ballet. In such instances, the presentation may take precedence over the content. The clothes are merely props or part of the cast.

3. Think of a fashion show and most people think of a moving presentation on live models on a catwalk or runway (the terms are interchangeable). But a fashion show can be very effective without any models. The clothes can be presented on static mannequins or body forms, among which the audience can wander. The big difference here is that the merchandise can be touched and examined close-up, something that is impossible during a conventional show, in which the impact is mainly visual and audial. This approach works especially well when your budget is limited, but it also suitable when you want a more intimate presentation. It also works well when the designer is on hand to talk about his or her clothes.

4. A fashion show can be part of a marketing campaign, to announce the arrival of a new designer, a new company or a new shop. Here, the aim is to make the most positive impression possible and – this is important – to ensure that your guests have something to take away with them to remember you by. This might be a catalogue, a brochure, a flyer, a simple postcard, a discount card to encourage them to shop with you, or a lavish goody bag. The ambition has to be that the audience contacts you after the show to learn more.

5. Once you are clear about why you are staging the event, you can start thinking about how you are going to execute it.

LEFT — The finishing touches are applied at London Collections: Men in 2013.

ABOVE — An image of a setting sun makes a striking backdrop to the Vivienne Westwood show in London for SS09 (Photo courtesy of My Beautiful City).

ABOVE — At London Fashion Week, the patterns in the Henry Holland collection are echoed in the patterned runway (Photo courtesy of My Beautiful City).

ABOVE — Neutral tones and straight-haired models bring unity to the Daks AW14 show at London Fashion Week.

BELOW — China-born Simon Gao sent models in blue and blue-grey shades for his AW14 show in London – and they all wore the same shoes.

GOING IT ALONE, OR A JOINT EFFORT?

——

Major international brands usually stage a show just for themselves, but many smaller events are put on by a group of companies or an alliance of like-minded people. A fashion school or college production will have many different designers that have to be accommodated. A show in a shopping mall or for a local shopping district probably will combine the efforts of several retailers who want to promote their stores. A catwalk presentation at a fashion exhibition will comprise outfits from a range of participating companies. Staging the show alone or putting it on in conjunction with someone else may require different approaches. More participants will always lead to more discussion before agreement is reached, but will increase the budget and share the workload.

1. Having a solo show means that you have, in theory, complete creative and artistic control. The ethos of your business can be expressed and transmitted to the audience in exactly the way you want. Every detail can be decided by you.

2. There are many advantages, however, to combining with other partners. The cost of the event is shared, as is the considerable workload and the responsibility. Two or more brains are often better than one for thinking up ideas.

3. Having other participants can also increase the appeal of your event, bringing in other guests that you might not be able to reach alone. The best idea is to have complementary partners, ones that mutually support each other.

4. Some partnerships obviously work well on the catwalk or runway, such as a clothing firm joining with a footwear or accessory producer. You might also think of a partner for off-runway activity, such as a local bar providing refreshments before and after the show itself, or a local beauty salon doing hair, make-up, manicures and pedicures for the models.

5. Having more than one participant can mean that the whole event is more of an experience, more memorable and more effective in its aims – but those aims need to be agreed upon from the start.

ABOVE — Sock it to me: A model ditches her shoes
during the Sister by Sibling AW14 show in London.

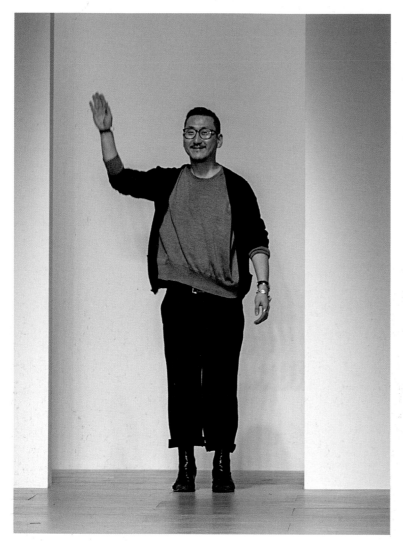 

ABOVE LEFT — Korean-born Eudon Choi acknowledges the applause at his AW14 show in London.

ABOVE RIGHT — Simon Gao still has the energy to run down the catwalk after his AW14 London presentation.

BELOW — At the Sibling show in London for AW14, the audience was seated a step up from the runway.

WHAT IS YOUR BUDGET?

———

Money makes the world go round, as the old song says, and it certainly makes a fashion show happen. Worldwide, there is a huge industry in events planning and sophisticated companies can provide the full package for staging your fashion show. Some have most or all of the services in-house, while others call in specialist firms for particular jobs such as building an elevated catwalk or setting up a lighting rig or building a bank of seating. This book is aimed that those who wish to do all or most of the work themselves, but in your planning it would be worth considering using specialist companies for some essential tasks.

1. By using the information in this book you can put together a reliable spreadsheet of costs for your event. Every professional show organizer stresses that the entire project from start to finish – which includes clearing up and following up after the event – needs to be rigorously planned and budgeted for.

2. A checklist of obvious costs might include: hire of venue; hire of equipment, such as stage, catwalk, lighting rig, public address system, seating; hiring of models, hairdressers, make-up artists, dressers; publicity costs, such as printing of posters to promote the event, email and social-media messages, construction of a website or web pages on your existing site; security and cloakroom staff if applicable; catering if you are offering food and drink; payment of helpers at the event; transport of clothes and accessories to and from the venue; goody bags (if they cannot be sourced for free); legal costs, which could include a licence to hold an event, public liability insurance, licence to play recorded music.

3. Remember that costs occur not only at the event. Professional models, hair and make-up artists and dressers will have to be paid to attend the fitting and rehearsal, which would normally be held on a different day.

ABOVE — A sumptuous venue for a show during London Collections: Men is made intimate by having only two rows of seating, then a few standing places at the rear.

LEFT — The power of repetition – using identical of very similar outfits – is a tried and tested device on the catwalk, as seen here in the Topman show at London Collections: Men for SS14.

ABOVE — The quiet before the excitement: the Tate Modern's Turbine
Hall was the venue for the Topshop Unique AW14 show at London
Fashion Week. Note the stepped arrangement for the banks of seating.

ABOVE — Food for thought: guests were fed and watered at the Topshop Unique AW14 show.

RIGHT — Edeline Lee reinforces her brand identity with a prominent logo at the end of her catwalk.

LOOKING FOR SPONSORS

___

Fashion is a sexy and desirable subject that attracts global brands to sponsor top-line events. For example, Mercedes-Benz has sponsored the official Fashion Weeks in New York, Berlin, Milan and London, in addition to supporting the Haute Couture and Prêt à Porter events in Paris. Organizers of smaller fashion shows should be alert to the possibilities of finding sponsors who can add value and prestige to their activities, as well as helping defray the costs.

1. The support of sponsors can come in the form of a financial contribution but is also provided via the provision of equipment or services for free. Many fashion design student collections benefit from fabric companies supplying the raw materials for free so, in a way, those fabric firms are underwriting the end-of-year catwalk shows. The credit the fabric suppliers receive on the show publicity helps promote their work to other designers and manufacturers that may like what they see and go and see what other designs the firm supplies. There is also often a sense of the company 'putting something back' into the industry by nurturing a new generation of talent.

2. In searching for a partner or sponsor, you should be asking, is this company appropriate to what I am trying to achieve? Is it a good fit with my event? And would my event and the audience it attracts be of benefit to the sponsor? Successful sponsorship always has two-way benefits.

3. You may be able to persuade specialist firms such as electrical contractors, audio engineers or video makers to provide their services for free or at a substantial discount. There are obvious synergies to be had by approaching cosmetic companies to supply make-up or local hairdressing salons to provide their stylists for the event. Usually, such partners are looking only for a credit in any pre-publicity, on the invitations and other collateral, at the show itself and in any post-show publicity.

4. A fashion show can become a hub for activity in a community. Complementary retailers, such as food stores or bars, could provide refreshments. A local printer might produce your invitations and programme for the event. A security firm may offer some staff to help with getting your audience in and out.

5. Obviously, an event that is raising money for charity might find it easier to attract sponsorship, but the important thing is to approach potential sponsors in plenty of time, not at the last minute, when you may appear desperate. Try and identify what the benefits are to them in sponsoring you, rather than pointing out the obvious benefits to yourself. Make sure you think of everything you need before approaching a potential sponsor; it's easy to ask for everything you need once, rather than going back a second or third time.

ABOVE — Local motor dealers are often pleased to be associated with a fashion event and can provide transport for VIPs.

RIGHT — Emerging designers, like those championed by the Fashion Scout organisation in London, are often attractive to sponsors.

ABOVE AND RIGHT—

Twice a year, the courtyard of the historic Somerset House on the banks of the River Thames in central London is transformed into the British Fashion Council's Catwalk Show Space for London Fashion Week, which attracts internationally recognized sponsors.

ABOVE — Cosmetics brands like L'Oréal are appropriate partners for fashion shows, as here at 2006 summer show for graduates of the Central St Martins school in London.

WHAT TYPE OF FASHION SHOW IS RIGHT FOR YOU?

—

The words 'fashion show' will conjure in most minds a straight, raised catwalk surrounded by an audience on two sides and a bank of photographers at the end of the runway. It is a classic configuration, but it is not the only way to stage a memorable and effective show. There are many other options that might better suit your aim, your budget, your timescale and your organizational abilities. The layout of the venue and the size of your audience will also influence which style is right for you.

1. The classic raised runway show works well if you have a large audience of more than a hundred people. As long as your seating arrangements are correct, it should allow the audience to have a good view of the clothes. The elevated platform immediately creates a sense of occasion and theatre. It easily allows several models to be on the catwalk at the same time, which keeps the show moving. But bear in mind you may not want too many models at once as this can become confusing.

2. Depending on the configuration of your venue and the size of the audience, you can have a low catwalk of perhaps 10cm (4in) off the ground, or have the models simply parade on a flat floor. Catwalks are available for hire in kit form, if your budget allows this. A parade of models at a lower level can create a more intimate feeling for your guests, literally allowing them to be closer to the action and the clothes. In this instance, the path of the models would still be defined by use of a carpet, perhaps.

3. A third option is a 'salon presentation', in which the models wander among the crowd, who may be standing or seated or a mixture of the two. Clearly, this is a more low-key and relaxed way of introducing your collection to its potential audience. It is often appropriate for smaller designers who do not have a large collection to exhibit, or for when the invited audience itself is quite small. This method also allows the audience to touch and examine the styles in greater detail.

4. The show can also be presented in the context of an entertainment, such as a dance-based performance or a piece of musical theatre. Having a high-energy show that is an entertainment rather than a chance to showcase the clothes is a popular option, especially with well-known designers, labels or retailers for which the show is a branding exercise to keep the name in the public eye. Staging such an event in a purpose-built theatre makes a lot of sense.

5. Many charity fashion shows are part of a larger social occasion such as a lunch or a dinner. Sometimes, a fixed catwalk might not be possible due to space reasons or because of problems with the diners all getting a good view. A popular solution is to have the models promenading around the tables, often while the host, hostess or a compere explains what they are wearing. In settings like this, music may be playing only softly in the background, or may not be used at all if a spoken commentary is being delivered.

ABOVE — A runway can be defined by something
as simple as a patterned floor covering.

ABOVE — A striking outfit needs to be seen in a simple, clean setting, as here at Pam Hogg in London for AW13.

RIGHT — Dramatic lighting will literally highlight a key item in a show.

ABOVE — A plain white background is very versatile and is especially effective for bright clothes, such as here from Christopher Raeburn in London for AW14.

WHICH DAY AND WHAT TIME OF DAY?

—

The fashion industry works to a regular timetable, which is why the big international fashion weeks always happen around the same time of year, twice a year. At major events, such as the fashion weeks (which, oddly enough, rarely last seven days), there can be between 100–200 shows and events to cram in, so the schedule is carefully worked out. The idea should be to make it easy for the fashion buyers and fashion writers to get to as many events as possible. If your show is part of a larger event, such as a local festival or a shopping mall's day of activity, it is important to consider how your event will dovetail with what else is going on. If your show will be a stand-alone one-off, your main consideration must be what's best for your target audience.

1. If your audience is a business audience, such as trade buyers or press, Tuesday, Wednesday and Thursday during the day is a good option. Monday tends to be a busy day in the office for retailers and Friday often sees them out visiting shops, so the mid-week slot is popular.

2. Top buyers and journalists are invited to many, many events and it can be hard to get them to come to small-scale events in the evening. You might have a better chance with a daytime slot.

3. If you are a shop owner wanting to stage a promotional show, the timing depends on your target audience. If your core customers are 'yummy mummies', something that avoids the school run timings would be appropriate. Busy mothers also have difficulty in giving up an evening.

4. If your target group is young people in work or students, then an evening event, say in a club, would obviously be an interesting option. It is important to check what else is going on in your vicinity. Often, picking a relatively quiet night can make your show a major attraction; indeed a club owner may be glad of you bringing in extra custom and so may offer the venue for free.

5. If your presentation is strong enough, it makes perfect sense to have it in the evening, maybe even on a Saturday night, to make it a real occasion for your target audience.

6. Bear in mind the time of year, too. Coming out on a warm summer's evening is obviously more appealing than venturing into a stormy winter's night.

ABOVE — Clever lighting picks out individual outfits as they are sent
down the runway at the AW14 Topshop Unique show in London.

LEFT — A live rockabilly trio provides the soundtrack for the static presentation by London-based Japanese Yasuko Furuta of Toga during London Fashion Week for AW14.

THE VENUE

—

The venue determines so much about the look and feel of your fashion show. Your original concept for the show might determine what sort of venue you look for. The options range from custom-built facilities that have existing useful installations (such as a theatre, school or college gymnasium, night club, hotel ballroom or conference centre) to places that you will have to adapt and work with. The deciding factor will be how much time, money, energy and expertise you have at your disposal. Another huge consideration is access – how easy or difficult will it be for your target audience to get to the venue? If they have to drive, can they park conveniently? Can taxis easily find the location?

1. Deciding on your expected attendance will assist you in choosing a venue. A cramped venue is unlikely to create the right atmosphere, but to have a small crowd 'lost' in a large venue is equally disappointing.

2. As well as the audience, it is essential that the venue can accommodate an adequate backstage area that has simple, safe and immediate access to the runway or presentation area. Managing the entire backstage process is the key to providing an excellent experience at a show (see page 122).

3. In the jargon of the show industry, a 'dry-hire venue' is one in which you take everything in – the stage, the seating, the lights, the production desk for the lighting and music, etc. It is essential that such a space has a reliable electrical supply. Has it got toilet facilities, or will you need to bring in portable toilets? Will it pass a health and safety check? Is it protected by the necessary public liability insurance?

4. In a 'wet-hire venue', you use the existing facilities and utilities and take in just the creative requirements, which could also include the stage, the seating, the lights, the production desk and so on.

5. The comfort of your guests during the show must be a high priority. Is the venue air-conditioned? Or does it need to be heated? How will the space feel when it has fifty, a hundred or 250 people in it?

6. Is natural light an advantage or a disadvantage? How will you close off natural light if it's not required?

7. Selecting a wacky and remote venue that has never seen a fashion event before may seem like a good idea, but how easy will it be for your guests to travel to the show? Or for all those involved to get the event together before the big day?

8. Ensure that wherever you stage your event you have all the necessary licences and permissions from the local authorities, all the required insurance (either directly or through the specialists you hire), and that you have conducted a thorough event safety plan. Specialist companies that are up-to-date with all the local requirements can do this last task for you.

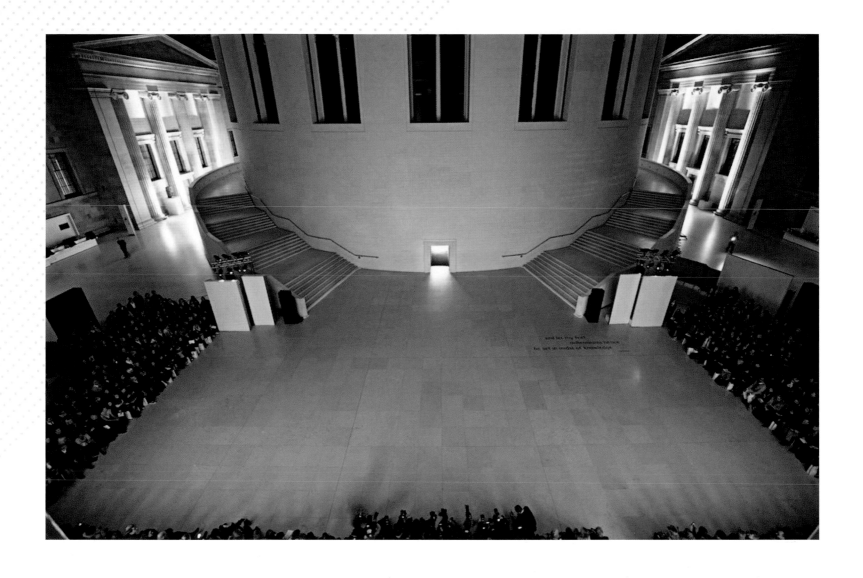

ABOVE — The audience at the British Museum awaits the start of the Alice Temperley show during London Fashion Week (Photo courtesy of My Beautiful City).

ABOVE — Thirty two models gather for the finale of the Alice Temperley show at the British Museum during London Fashion Week (Photo courtesy of My Beautiful City).

LEFT — The Turbine Hall of the Tate Modern is transformed into a modernist runway for the Topshop Unique show during London Fashion Week for AW14.

ABOVE — A simple yet attractive static presentation by Whistles during the AW14 London Fashion Week.

RIGHT — London-based Pam Hogg uses a wide runway in London for her AW14 collection.

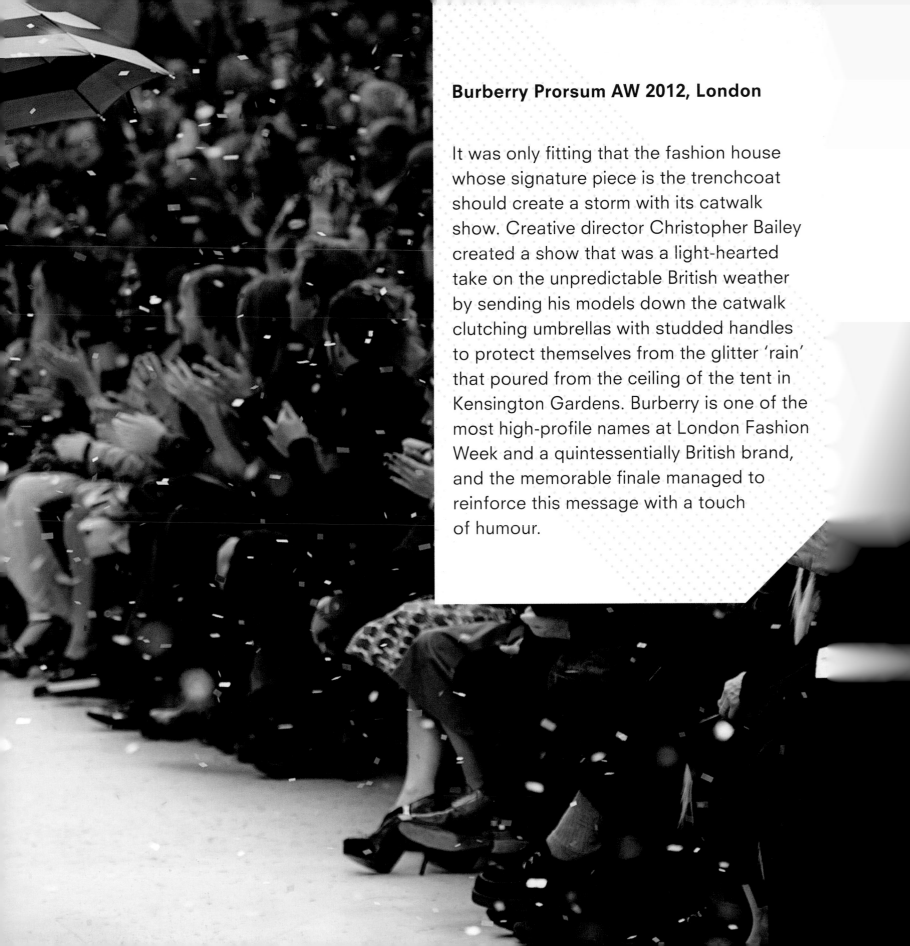

Burberry Prorsum AW 2012, London

It was only fitting that the fashion house whose signature piece is the trenchcoat should create a storm with its catwalk show. Creative director Christopher Bailey created a show that was a light-hearted take on the unpredictable British weather by sending his models down the catwalk clutching umbrellas with studded handles to protect themselves from the glitter 'rain' that poured from the ceiling of the tent in Kensington Gardens. Burberry is one of the most high-profile names at London Fashion Week and a quintessentially British brand, and the memorable finale managed to reinforce this message with a touch of humour.

SHOULD YOU HOLD THE SHOW INDOORS OR OUTDOORS?

―

Many places in the world are blessed with a climate that is both pleasant and reliable. Other regions are less fortunate, which is why, for example, show organizers in northern Europe are not keen on outdoor events. The weather is just too unpredictable. Whether held indoors or outdoors, the principles of staging a successful show remain the same. There must be a good backstage area, the clothes must be easy to see by the audience, and the guests themselves ought to be comfortable and safe.

1. Ensure that any outside location has ground that is stable enough to take a raised catwalk, if you are using one, and that there is an adequate and reliable source of electrical power. Any power cables need to be safely out of the way of guests and models alike.

2. If you are in a sunny climate, consider where the sun will be at the time of your show. Try to avoid having half your audience or the models squinting into the sun.

3. A halfway house for an outdoor show is to hold it in a temporary structure such as a marquee, which can be of considerable proportions. Apart from the cost implications, consider also how the backstage area, the catwalk itself and the seating arrangements will work within a temporary structure. Will a temporary floor be required? How will the lighting be delivered? How can the temperature in the marquee be regulated?

4. If the circumstances are right, an outdoor 'salon presentation' could be a very effective method of showing your clothes. Having models walking among the guests would give any garden party a fashionable slant.

5. If going outdoors, think also about the PA system you would need. To be effective, it's likely to be bigger and more powerful than one used in an enclosed space indoors.

ABOVE — Back-to-back seats in the middle of a rectangular floor
provide more "front row" places and create a circular runway (Photo
courtesy of My Beautiful City).

ABOVE — No need for a lighting rig for this sunny rooftop show by New York-based designed Benjamin Cho.

ABOVE — Even a derelict site can be brought into use as a venue (as long as it passes the Health & Safety regulations).

ABOVE — London design duo Tata Naka (Georgian-born identical twins Tamara and Natasha Surguladze) are celebrated for their bright prints and they include clashing patterns in the wall and floor of their AW14 presentation.

ABOVE — Lily Cole dances at the start of a Vivienne Westwood show. Note how the red lighting creates a dramatic atmosphere (Photo courtesy of My Beautiful City).

Fendi, AW 2007, China

Karl Lagerfeld made quite an impact when he used a section of the Great Wall of China to showcase his collection for Fendi. Along with sending his models to walk down a majestic World Heritage site Lagerfeld also jetted in 500 guests from all over the world, meaning the show costs came to over $10 million.

THE STRUCTURE OF THE SHOW

Part commercial enterprise, part artistic endeavour, a successful fashion show should be an experience for the audience. It should be viewed like a theatrical play or a rock concert, with a carefully considered opening, middle and finale. Every piece of merchandise you show should be there for a reason; it should work singly and also in the context of the other items you are presenting. The best shows are like a little story.

1. Start with a blank piece of paper and jot down how you envisage the show working. What outfit would be right to open the show? It should have impact, of course, but it should probably not be the best piece in your collection. That ought to have final appearance.

2. Identify how many elements you want in the show. There should be a different approach if they are all in the same category (i.e. all evening dresses or all jeans outfits) than if you are showing a wide selection of wardrobe favourites. What is the story you are trying to tell?

3. If the important thing is to let the audience see and enjoy the clothes themselves, the restrained and conventional approach of having models walking up and down the catwalk is probably the best one.

4. If the idea is to have more of an entertainment, then a lively dance-based presentation could be more appropriate.

5. A continuous line of single models walking down the catwalk with a suitable gap between them is an effective way in which to showcase a collection, but variety can be added by sending down two or more models at once. The width of the runway will determine how many people can be seen at once, but varying the number gives pace and rhythm to the presentation. A good show should seem relaxed, even nonchalant, but it takes a lot of planning to achieve this.

6. Remember when planning what will happen on the catwalk that you also have to plan what will take place simultaneously backstage. You have to ensure that you have enough models to satisfy your plans and that they each have time to change from one scene to their next.

7. If both sexes are featured in the show, consider how best to integrate them. A female scene followed by a male scene followed by a joint scene might work. How you want the show to look will be determined by the clothes – in many cases, they should be the starting point for everything at the event.

8. The overall performance will be a combination of the input from the stylist, who creates the look for the models, the choreographer, who determines what happens on the catwalk itself, and the person who selects the music, which is the obvious complement to the visual impact.

LEFT — Note how the wall decorations at Edeline Lee's AW14 London show echo the colours and prints of her collection.

ABOVE — A lighting rig should put the emphasis on the catwalk, leaving the audience in relative darkness.

LEFT — Modern technology enables the backstage team to see all the proceedings on the catwalk to communicate with the team at the front side of Jamie Wei Huang's AW14 show in London.

ABOVE — Ensure that the spacing of your show allows each outfit to be seen clearly by the audience, as here at Pam Hogg's show for AW13 in London.

BELOW — Remember not to give your guests too much to look at all at once.

THE LENGTH OF THE SHOW

There is an old showbiz adage that says you should always leave the audience wanting more. Probably the biggest mistake made in amateur fashion shows is to have them running for too long. Despite the massive amount of work that goes into staging a show, professional organizers suggest that the best length for a presentation is just 15–20 minutes. Most strongly recommend not doing anything more than 35 minutes.

1. Like a great pop song, a great fashion show should be short, snappy and exciting. In the case of a designer, a fashion brand or a retailer, the idea should be to give just a flavour of what you do, not show every single item you have in your collection. Editing the show is vital for its success. If the audience members like what they see, they will seek you out to learn more.

2. Even in a short show, there should be a structure, which involves creating an engaging 'rhythm' that builds up to a finale. Resist the temptation to overfill the catwalk with models and merchandise. Very often, less is more.

3. If more than one individual or company is involved in the fashion show, it can be tricky to keep the presentation to an ideal length, but try to reduce everything down to the strongest, most relevant looks that work together.

4. One of the most challenging tasks of the show organizer is to edit the presentation down to a manageable length. The more time spent carefully planning and taking things out will almost certainly result in a better, more effective and more successful event.

ABOVE — A catwalk show can present a variety of looks, as seen here at Christopher Raeburn's presentation in London for AW14.

LEFT — Some outfits, such as this dress by London-based Marios Schwab, are so impressive that they require no fancy tricks on the catwalk.

ABOVE — The clothes are different but the models look alike in
Canada-born Jean-Pierre Braganza's AW14 show in London.

ABOVE — A parade of the entire cast of models, as here at Simone Rocha's AW14 show in London, is the traditional sign-off for a catwalk presentation.

THE LAYOUT OF A CLASSIC CATWALK

The T-shaped runway is the most familiar catwalk configuration. It is popular because it allows space for models to come on and off at the same time on the wide part at the top, while the runway itself takes the show literally into the audience. The bar of the T also allows a number of models to be presented together in a line, adding a sense of drama to the presentation.

1. There needs, of course, to be some sort of wall or barrier between the catwalk and backstage. A common configuration is to have a wall occupying the centre of the stage with two other walls on each side set back about 1m (3¼ft). From the audience, this almost looks like a continuous wall, but it allows the models on and off the stage through the gaps on each side.

2. Another version reverses this configuration, so that the models appear through an arch behind which is the back wall. It is important that the models can enter and exit the catwalk area easily – the audience should not be aware of how this is happening.

3. The height and width of the back walls will depend on your venue. Catwalks and back walls are all available for hire in kit form. Normally, the back panels would be about 2.5m (or 8¼ft high), but there is no set rule.

4. Having a plain back wall at the top of the T is useful as you can project information onto it that you want your audience to see, such as the name of the designer or the sponsors.

5. Projections are especially useful if there are several designers, brands or retailers involved in the show. The projection can change when products from each appear.

6. The back wall can also be used as a screen if you choose to run video footage of the show as it happens or other visual imagery that can enhance your fashion show.

7. The back wall can be decorated to set the mood of your show, or it can feature something like theatrical scenery. Quite a modest design can have a powerful effect.

8. To make an impact, a catwalk should be at least 6m (6yd) long, allowing a model to take six or seven steps before reaching the end of it. You must calculate what the venue and your budget can stand. Huge professional fashion shows can have catwalks of up to 50m (54yd) or more in length, but that would be very ambitious for a small-scale event.

9. The far end of the catwalk is the place usually reserved for photographers and camera teams. Depending on the number you are expecting, their area might need to be stepped so that all can have a clear view of the catwalk. Ideally the photographers should be at the same height as the catwalk.

ABOVE — Putting guests in the middle of the floor creates a circular runway and gets more people nearer the action.

ABOVE — California-based Michelle Mason presented her Signature
Collection in spring 2004 in a brightly-lit tunnel in Los Angeles.

ABOVE — A single spotlight picks out a single model during the Daks AW14 show in London.

OTHER CATWALK CONFIGURATIONS

The venue and the size of the audience will determine if you can send your models down something other than a conventional runway. It is perfectly logical to have them parade in a circle or a figure of eight or some other configuration. Your primary concern should be: can all my guests see all the featured outfits?

1. Logistically, the requirement is to send the model out from the backstage area and then return to the backstage area to change into the next outfit.

2. It would be possible (although not recommended!) to have two backstage areas at each end of a complicated route, but be aware that you would probably be doubling the number of dressers and wardrobe staff you would need.

3. A longer and more complicated catwalk will also add to your budget if you are building it from scratch or hiring it.

4. It is easier to have an unconventional runway when you are sending your models along a flat floor.

5. If you have enough models, you could send each of them out in just one outfit, negating the need for them to return to the backstage area. They could set off from backstage but finish their promenade somewhere else, if the venue layout permits.

LEFT — Models line up for the dress rehearsal at the Jamie Wei Huang AW14 show in London.

RIGHT — Allow time for a full dress rehearsal so that your models can get used to wearing high shoes and unusual clothes, like this outfit by Patrick Li in the Royal College of Art Graduate Fashion Show in London in June 2011.

ABOVE LEFT — A shiny floor gives yet another visual angle.

ABOVE RIGHT — A model wearing designs by Anna Schwamborn circles the audience at the Royal College of Art Graduate Fashion Show in June 2011.

BELOW — A neat seating arrangement makes excellent use of a relatively small area for a Vivienne Westwood show in London.

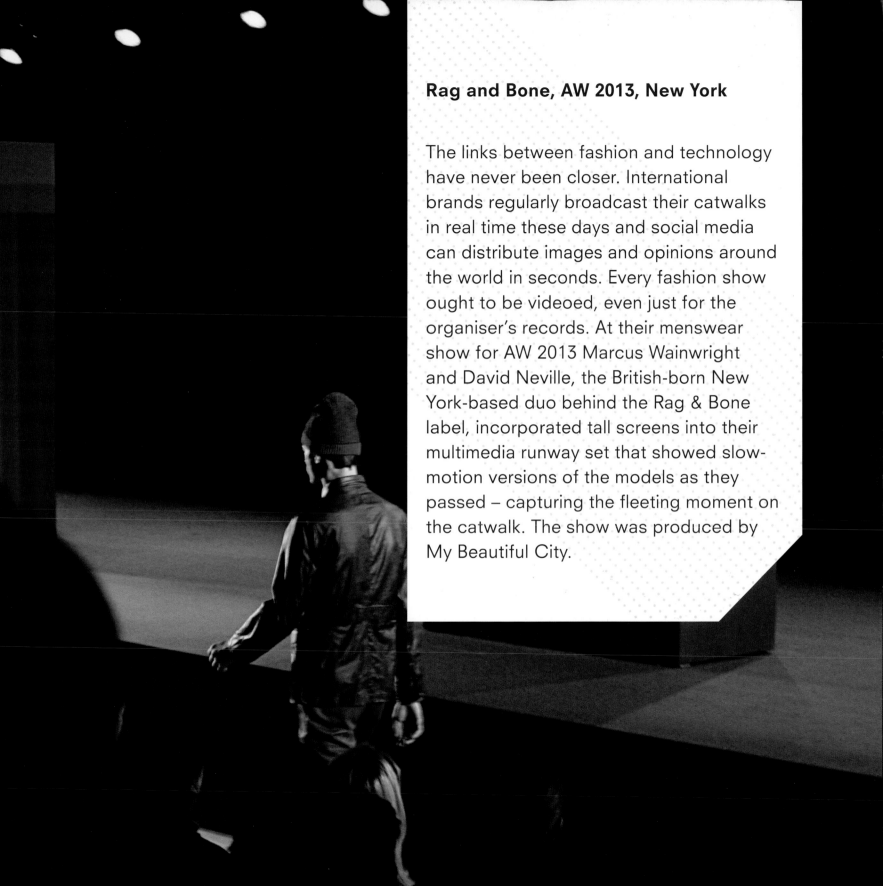

Rag and Bone, AW 2013, New York

The links between fashion and technology have never been closer. International brands regularly broadcast their catwalks in real time these days and social media can distribute images and opinions around the world in seconds. Every fashion show ought to be videoed, even just for the organiser's records. At their menswear show for AW 2013 Marcus Wainwright and David Neville, the British-born New York-based duo behind the Rag & Bone label, incorporated tall screens into their multimedia runway set that showed slow-motion versions of the models as they passed – capturing the fleeting moment on the catwalk. The show was produced by My Beautiful City.

CALCULATING THE BEST CONFIGURATION FOR YOUR SHOW

The expected number of your audience will largely determine the size of your catwalk and the style of your seating. The two options are essentially to put the models at a higher level so that they can be seen better, or to lift up the audience. Think of how the seats in a cinema or theatre are raked to allow all of the audience to get a good view. You have to achieve the same effect.

1. Professional organizers advise that you should have only two rows of seats on the same level. After that, your seats must be raked or tiered in some way so that each subsequent row is higher than the one in front.

2. One idea to give everyone a good view is to go for a large venue so that you can have the seating arranged such that almost everyone is in the front row. This may be less expensive than building a seating bank, but it could mean the occasion lacks a sense of theatre.

3. Another often-used solution is to have a long, essentially circular, walkway, so that the models move through the audience. The guests' seating is normally arranged in two lines to define the edges of the catwalk.

4. Raked seating can be hired and should pass all necessary safety regulations.

5. Qualified carpenters could build a framework for seating, but the cost of making a temporary structure may be more than hiring ready-made banks of seating.

6. It is quite usual to have less important guests, such as friends, standing at the rear of the seats.

ABOVE — A large number of models demand a long runway so that they can be
accommodated, as here at the Topshop Unique show at the AW14 London Fashion Week.

HOW MUSIC CAN CREATE
THE RIGHT ATMOSPHERE

——

All five senses can be delighted at a fashion show. You could offer canapés or drinks for your guests. Or spray the room with fragrance just before the audience arrives. If you are showing a fashion collection you have designed, you could put tiny samples of the fabric you have used on your running orders you hand out to your guests. The visual delight will be your show. But the most impactful sensory delight after the visual should be the audial. Music will help create just the right atmosphere at your event. Choose it wisely.

1. The quality of the sound system cannot be overestimated. If you have to hire it, borrow it or buy it, go for the best you can.

2. The desire is to create a consistent, ambient sound that fills the entire venue equally. So avoid having a bank of speakers that someone has to sit next to.

3. The music should be controlled from the front of the stage, so that the person controlling it has a perfect view of the proceedings on the catwalk.

4. The choice of music will be decided during the early discussions about the image of the show. Depending on the length of your show, you could choose just one long track or keep to one style of music, or have various tracks to complement different scenes in the show.

5. You can produce a pre-recorded selection of music (allow for slightly more music than you think you need, in case a scene overruns), or you can have your sound person mix the edit on site as the show is going on – but obviously you need an experienced DJ to ensure a faultless performance.

6. Most shows would use recorded music, but an ambitious idea could be to have a live ensemble playing. It could make a memorable occasion (if you have enough rehearsal time…).

7. For very intimate presentations, with a small audience, you could do without music at all. This might work if you are a designer who wants to explain to your invitees about your collection. It could also be appropriate, for example, if you are a shop keeper who wants to tell the audience about the clothes you are showing them, explaining how items work together or revealing details that cannot be seen simply from the outside.

ABOVE — Live music gives a show a special attitude, whether classical, as here at the Erdem SS14 show in London (above), or rockabilly, as provided by the trio at the Toga presentation for AW14 (above right).

ABOVE — Sergio Pizzorno, guitarist with the rock band Kasabian, mixes the tunes at a presentation by menswear designer Aitor Throup in London.

ABOVE — A sophisticated approach would synchronise in advance the lighting and sound tracks for the show, as seen at the Turkish designer Hakan Akkaya's show in 2013.

ABOVE RIGHT — Live classical music was used at the Erdem SS14 show in London.

HOW TO LIGHT A FASHION SHOW RUNWAY

Well before setting up the lights on any fashion show, it is best to draw a plan of the stage and mark the location of lights. This makes it easier to set up, especially if you are using an outside company for the lights. You will almost always need lighting up along the edge of the runway. Additional spotlights will help showcase the clothes at certain points on the runway.

1. Based on your budget, research the cost of different options for lighting. You may need to hire lights, rigging and an experienced crew, which should be covered by its own insurance. It would be inadvisable to try to set up a lighting rig yourself.

2. Visit and look over the location if the runway is already set up. Make detailed notes of its length, width and design (a single lane, a T-shape and so on). This should help you determine the best place for each light.

3. Draw a diagram of the runway, with measurements, and with the placement of lighting at strategic places. Give each placement of a light a number. If there is a problem with a light, the numbering system will help you identify it.

4. Use masking tape on the runway to indicate the location of a light. Do this on both sides of the runway.

5. On the rigging system, fix the spotlights where you think they should be positioned. Turn them on to test them. Any changes to position can be made during the rehearsals when you are fine-tuning your show concept.

6. Modern LED (light-emitting diode) lights are much more efficient than the traditional filament lights, which used to throw off huge amounts of heat. But be aware that even LED bulbs still become hot, so do not have any decorations, hangings, coverings and so on too near the lights.

7. Like changes in music, changes in the lighting during the show itself should be made from the production desk located within the audience space (but obviously not obscuring the view of guests or photographers).

8. If you are using the lights already installed in a venue, such as a restaurant for a lunchtime show, drama can be created by dimming the lights and having the models illuminated by a 'follow spot', a spot light that is manually operated and can be directed to follow a model around.

9. Using a professional entertainment setting, such as a local theatre or nightclub, can give you access to a sophisticated light system and professional staff who know how to get the most out of it.

10. Remember that if your show is for purely commercial or selling reasons, your audience needs to see the clothes, so a bright, consistent coverage of light could be your best strategy.

11. If the show is more of an event or entertainment, more dramatic and dynamic lighting will add to the atmosphere.

12. The lighting team might well also handle other elements of your event, such as projections you may wish to show on the wall of the stage. This is particularly helpful if yours is a multi-designer or multi-brand show. You need to inform the audience about which participant they are looking at, and projections can do so effectively but without distracting from the activity on the catwalk. (You can also make announcements over the PA system, of course).

13. Consider simple lighting effects, such as a 'black light' or ultra-violet light, which could be used sparingly during the show to add a moment of drama.

RIGHT — Simple yet powerful, spotlights on each side of the runway make a dramatic effect for Australian designer Alex Perry's SS08 show.

ABOVE — At London Fashion Week, Marjan Pejoski and Sasko Bezovski, the design duo behind KTZ, used a versatile lighting rig to illuminate their catwalk.

ABOVE — Models find the right spotlights during rehearsals for the Mercedes-Benz Fashion Week in Istanbul for AW14.

ABOVE RIGHT — A spectacular rainbow effect light display decorates the runway for the Zimmermann SS 2003 during Mercedes Fashion in Sydney.

ABOVE AND LEFT — Mirrored 'shelves' create a visually interesting platform for the models at the static presentation for Whistles AW14 during London Fashion Week.

ABOVE — Lighting engineers position the spots for a Vivienne Westwood
show (Photo courtesy of My Beautiful City).

Matthew Williamson First show, London, September 1997

In 1998 Matthew Williamson, a young graduate of Central St Martins, showed his debut collection 'Electric Angels' during London Fashion Week, following the advice of Plum Sykes at Vogue magazine. He managed to persuade friends Kate Moss, Helena Christensen and Jade Jagger to model for him and the collection, for SS1998, was an immediate success.

HOW TO PUBLICIZE A PUBLIC EVENT

Some events are strictly private and very exclusive. Others are aimed at a wider audience and need to be publicized. Promoting the event before it happens is a great way of increasing consumer demand if you are organizing a charity event or an entertainment. Depending on the age of your target audience, you might wish to concentrate on promoting through social media or relying on more traditional methods such as posters, flyers and press advertisements.

1. It is good to promote the event publicly about 4–6 weeks before the actual date. Further ahead and many people do not want to commit. Nearer the date and people may have their diary filled.

2. Social media is the fastest, cheapest and most far-reaching method of reaching a target audience, but as well as just stating the fact (purpose of event, date, time and venue) ensure that you include contact details for booking tickets.

3. If your budget allows, creating a simple website is a very good way of informing a large number of people about what you are doing and why, where and when it is, and how they can become involved.

4. In any publicity, make sure that you include recognition of your sponsors and supporters. Include also reliable contact details for yourself in case people want more information.

LEFT — Photographers train their lenses on a model at Jamie Wei Huang's show in London.

RIGHT — Spanish fashion brand Mango provided long-stemmed roses for front-row guests at its SS 2009 show during London Fashion Week.

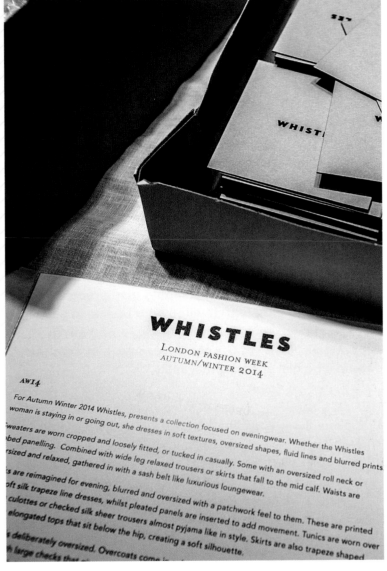

OPPOSITE — Leopard-skin patterned skateboards are ideal props for London-based Katie Eary's bright menswear for SS14.

ABOVE — Kanye West's invitation to the Louis Vuitton menswear show for AW 2009 in Paris.

ABOVE RIGHT — Whistles put together an information sheet on its collection for guests to its AW14 show in London.

ABOVE — An intimate show for E Tautz during London Collections:
Men gives everyone a close-up of the clothes.

ABOVE — Crowds gather outside Somerset
House for the London Fashion Week shows.

HOW TO SET UP YOUR FRONT ROW AND REST OF AUDIENCE

Everyone would like to be in the front row at a fashion show, so you must organize yours carefully, keeping several things in mind at the same time. Of course, it's the place for your most important guests, but how you arrange those guests will influence how successful the event is for them and for you.

1. When planning the runway and the room, work with venue staff to make sure you have the largest possible number of front row seats. Ensure all your high profile guests are on the front row.

2. Buy or hire the most comfortable seats you can afford for the front row (and the rest of the room if you can). Place the front row seats along the runway to maximize all the observation space. VIPs should have an unobstructed view. Attempt to give the people in the other rows the best sight lines, too.

3. Draw up a seating plan to seat VIPs, celebrities and press in a sequence that is harmonious. If you know of guests that are friends and colleagues, seat them together. Avoid putting editors who are bitter rivals or retail buyers who do not like each other in close proximity.

4. The best seats are at the far end of the catwalk, from where the full procession down the runway can be enjoyed, although if you have photographers at the event they must be positioned so they can have an unobstructed view.

5. For convenience, all blocks of seats, rows of seats and individual seats should be clearly identified. Your audience could be a mixture of designated seats, such as for important guests, and sit-where-you like areas, which are filled on a first come-first served basis. It is a nice touch when a VIP seat is marked with the person's name.

ABOVE — Anna Wintour, editor-in-chief of American Vogue, on the front row of Tom Ford's show for SS14 during London Fashion Week.

OPPOSITE— Bright young things: the Erdem show in London for SS14 attracts (from left) Pixie Geldof, Daisy Lowe, Laura Bailey, Poppy Delevingne, Alexa Chung and Laura Carmichael.

ABOVE — The front row gets a close encounter with a creation by Pam Hogg in London for AW14.

HOW BIG A CREW WILL YOU NEED?

As will be obvious to anyone reading this book, even small fashion shows require a lot of manpower (or womanpower!) to make them happen. A well-prepared, well-rehearsed, adequately numbered team will always produce a more satisfying event than too few people with too little preparation. The responsibilities of the crew can be divided between those that involve the show production and those that involve the audience. A professional event organizer could involve show producers, directors, choreographers, production managers, health and safety managers, stylists, backstage personnel, event coordinators, set designers, planners and technicians in specialist areas.

1. Looking at things from the guests' view, think about who will greet them at the door, check their invitation and see them to their seats. Consider if you will need any security to prevent uninvited gate crashers.

2. Consider the security aspect also if you are charging an entrance fee on the door, as often happens at a charity show or a show that is part of a night's entertainment at a club. Will you accept debit and credit cards, or will it be cash only? How will you look after the cash?

3. Make sure you have enough staff on the door to get your guests in quickly. A VIP entrance or line might be appropriate. It is good practice to keep everything running on time. If you say 'Doors open 7pm', make sure that they do.

4. Security staff and checkers-in at professional shows used to be called 'the clipboard mafia'. They would check off names from pre-printed lists held on a clipboard but, these days, iPads and other tablet devices are common – but they are used to do exactly the same job.

5. Be prepared for how to deal with the situation if a guest turns up with a friend or three and wants them to come in, too. If your venue is expected to be at full capacity, you may have to turn people away.

6. If your event is preceded and/or followed by drinks, you will probably need a cloakroom for guests' coats, bags and so on.

7. It would be usual at a large show for some staff to look after only media and photographers, while others would take care of the other guests. Photographers need to get into the venue in plenty of time to set up their equipment.

8. Once in the venue, guests need to be shown to their seats. Beware of cramming the seating too close together to save space – it makes it difficult for latecomers to squeeze past those already in their seats.

9. Important technical staff for the event, such as the people controlling the music and lighting, would probably be set up at the front of the stage so that they can see what's going on, but you do not want them occupying prime viewing space. That should be reserved for the invitees.

10. You need to have at least one person who is responsible for communicating from front-of-house to backstage. This will be most easily achieved through a personal radio system.

11. Backstage, the key people in charge are the wardrobe mistress, who is in charge of getting the clothes on the models and the models on the catwalk, and the 'show caller', who stands immediately backstage and sends the models out at the correct time.

LEFT — Last-minute finishing touches are applied at the Whistles AW14 static presentation.

ABOVE — Models in their own clothes, but with their hair already arranged in the same style, prepare for a rehearsal at the Jamie Wei Huang show in London.

ABOVE — Models wear plain white gowns while their hair is styled and make-up is applied at the Fred Butler show for SS13.

Anya Hindmarch, SS14, London

British designer Anya Hindmarch's SS14
show at Central Hall, Westminster, London,
started conventionally enough, with
models striding the runway clutching her
latest handbags. But then dozens of bags
on wires began to 'float' down from the
starry ceiling cloth before rising up again
on their supporting wires. To complete
the effect, the final two models appeared
wearing waist harnesses attached to wires
that swept them above the catwalk as the
ethereal soundtrack reached its gentle
crescendo. The airborne spectacle was
described by Vogue as being like 'Cirque
du Soleil for handbags'.

HOW TO SELECT THE CLOTHES

Designer shows aside, the clothes used in smaller fashion shows are often assembled with very little notice, requiring a certain flexibility, steady nerve and even temperament on the part of the show's stylist, who is responsible for pulling all the clothes and accessories together. If you are borrowing clothes from shops, the retailers will not want to part with them until the last possible moment. Essential pieces that you were expecting might be sold in advance of the show, or not be available in the right size or colour at the last minute. The stylist is responsible for deciding on the overall look of the whole show and will brief hairdressers and make-up artists to ensure that the look is cohesive.

1. Have a clear written brief: the stylist must understand the precise purpose and aim of the show. Ultimately, the stylist is to reflect the image the client or show organiser wishes to present and to sell their concept or range of clothes.

2. When putting together the look and running order of the show, familiarize yourself with the range of clothes on offer and see what stands out as being of interest so that you can draw up a wish list. You or your stylist may have ideas for a number of different stories that could create your desired effect. It is quite easy to become either overwhelmed by the range of choice on offer, or to allow one story to dominate so that you have a mass of outfits in one theme, but virtually none for others. Clothes selection is all about maintaining a balance and contributing to the dramatic impact of the event.

3. If you are using a stylist, ensure that he or she shows you the clothes and accessories they are collecting or considering in plenty of time. Communication is the key to avoiding any arguments near the deadline.

4. Don't overlook the value of basic pieces, such as white shirts or black T-shirts that can help to provide a cohesive element across a range of styles. Overestimate rather than underestimate your selection in this area.

5. Keep an eye out for a few show stoppers when you are selecting clothes for the show. You need stand-alone pieces that provide a real visual feast or provoke comment. Plan these into the running order carefully.

6. Bear in mind that you are looking to present a cohesive story, so a group of outfits must work together, not fight each other. In each story you are selling a look that the audience should be able to clearly understand and translate.

7. Contact companies who might provide accessories well in advance, as no one likes to feel as though they are a last-minute choice. Call in to make a basic selection as early as you can, explaining your anticipated requirements, although you may have to provide final details such as model shoe sizes

quite late in the proceedings. Establish in advance whether models or members of the audience can buy any pieces they take a particular shine to. Don't forget to source plenty of such basic but essential items as hosiery. Be prepared to have spares in case these are damaged during costume changes.

8. Once you have made a selection of clothes, arrange them in a rough running order. Each section of the show should work as a cohesive whole with a clear message, even when you are working across market sectors and age groups. Traditionally, shows start with the more casual message. Eveningwear comes towards the end of the show and a wedding dress, if you are featuring one, last of all. Any show should end with a visual highpoint. It is a good idea to photograph your outfits as you select them, ideally, but not necessarily, on a model, so that you can check what the visual impact will be of the scenes individually and collectively in sequence. Be prepared to make changes from your original concept if the clothes you are using dictate it.

9. If you are staging a fashion show to promote, say, a fashion store or website, ensure that you have plenty of stock for the garments you show. This consideration can make it difficult to plan a 'selling' show a long time in advance.

10. If possible, arrange for the models to try on the clothes in advance of the dress rehearsal. It is surprising how often certain outfits do not work so well on one model as another, or simply do not fit. Your models may all be theoretically the same size, but nevertheless physical variations – such as longer bodies, bigger shoulders, skinny legs and so on – can dictate what looks best on whom. You should also get the models to try on the preferred accessories to make sure that hats, shoes, belts and so on all fit and look good.

ABOVE — Special pieces and accessories are often created just for the catwalk show as with these over-sized mittens and balaclava for the AW13 show for Sibling in London.

11. Work out the final running order of clothes on specific models, making sure that your schedule gives them sufficient time to change between appearances.

12. When you know who is wearing what and in what sequence, you must arrange each rail. Each outfit must be clearly grouped together with accessories. When items such as shoes are shared between models, these must be kept separately, but detailed on the rail so that the dresser and model knows where to find them. Professional show organizers hang a photograph of the model in his or her precise outfit on the clothes rail to reduce the risk of a mix up.

13. If you are using new shoes, protect the sole of each shoe with masking tape or a custom-made reusable sole cover to protect it from scuffing so that it still can be sold after the show.

14. The stylist should run through the clothes with each dresser, highlighting any designs that are complex in construction or fastening.

15. The stylist needs to be out front to see the rehearsal and make sure that everything looks as good as it can.

16. During the show, the stylist should stand immediately beside the entrance to the catwalk, so that each model and their outfit can be checked before they go on.

17. When the show is finished the stylist should be responsible for making sure all borrowed clothes, accessories and props are returned in good order to the suppliers promptly.

ABOVE — A strong outfit can create a dramatic statement all on its own, as seen here in a show by London-based Jean-Pierre Braganza.

LEFT — It is effective to group similar outfits together in scenes, as London designer firm Mascot did for its SS13 show. Everything was then shown together for the finale.

HOW TO SELECT YOUR MODELS

A successful fashion show has a theme or a point of view. In the case of an event for an individual designer, this theme might echo the inspiration for his or her collection. It could be a historical period, a foreign country or an inspirational pop star, but in any case the entire production might be designed to tie in with this theme. Your choice of models should, therefore, reflect your theme. You might want all of them to look the same or you may wish to use a variety of ages, shapes and sizes. If you are organizing the event yourself, you will choose the models, but if you are using outside help, such as a show producer, a choreographer, or a stylist, a collaborative approach will be needed so that everyone has an input and is happy with the decision.

1. Professional models can be expensive, especially if they are established 'names'. They will have an enviable gloss and poise, but they may not take a small show very seriously and they may make the rest of your models look lacklustre in comparison. Remember – you will need them for the rehearsals as well as the actual show.

2. If your budget allows you to use professional models, always deal with reputable model agencies. They may be eager to have new models gain catwalk experience, so you may be able to persuade them to work for you at a reduced rate.

3. Of course the models – who are invariably referred to as 'girls' or 'boys', whatever their ages – have to be the right proportions for the clothes you want them to wear, but most important of all is that they can walk well down the runway. So you need to hold a casting at which you will invite far more models than you need and select the best.

4. Get each of them to walk up and down in front of you and ensure that they move smoothly and elegantly and with the right 'attitude'. Do not spend much time considering each of them. If you have doubts that they are what you want, they are probably not going to be right for you. (Obviously, the ability to walk well is not so important if you are having a static display or a presentation in which the models quietly interact with your audience.)

5. At the casting, get the models to wear the sort of footwear you will want them to wear during the show. The person who can walk well in trainers might not perform so convincingly in stilettos or heavy winter boots.

6. If you have made your collection all in one sample size, then you will require all your models to be the same size. A uniform look can be achieved by selecting models that are all the same types, such as blue-eyed blondes, or long-haired brunettes, but your look can also be achieved by using wigs and the same make-up on everyone.

7. If you use professional models, ensure that you have an agreement with the model agency that they can be photographed during the show and that you can use those images afterwards in your publicity, press packs, on your own website, etc. Some agencies may ask for more money for this, so bring up the subject early and be prepared to negotiate.

8. The antithesis of the uniform approach is to have a varied mix of models. This strategy is often used by independent boutiques that attract a wide range of customers. They often use their own shop staff, who can be widely different ages, shapes and sizes. Presenting your show in this way can make it more realistic and inclusive and is certainly recommended if you want to make immediate follow-up sales.

LEFT — A simple gallery of the models helps everyone backstage identify who is who.

9. If you decide to use non-professional models, select people with at least a slightly extrovert personality. As well as looking good in the clothes and moving well, they should really want to be on the runway. A lively group of friends or colleagues obviously having fun will really add to the show atmosphere.

10. Another option is to mix professional models with amateurs, or to mix 'walking' models with professional dancers. It all depends on the theme for your show and how you want to choreograph it. Remember, though, if you are working with dancers, that their proportions are radically different to those of models – they are smaller and more muscular, so sample sizes may not fit.

11. There should be no shortage of volunteers for modelling at a fashion college. Often, design students appear in each other's shows. If you can get enough people to model for you, it could be that you do not have to make any costume changes. If you have 20 outfits and 20 models, you will have a less complicated task backstage.

12. If you are working with amateur models, remind them that they will need to bring a dressing gown with them, as well as neutral underwear. Models should wear flesh-coloured underwear, as this will work under both dark and pale outfits, and they should wear smooth pants that won't leave any kind of VPL (visible panty line). A model should change into their dressing gown before hair and make-up is done, and should remove any underwear or socks that might leave undesirable marks on their bodies.

13. It can be helpful if models bring some of their own shoes with them, in case there are not enough shoes or they do not fit. Nothing increases the odds of a calamitous catwalk fall like a pair of ill-fitting shoes.

14. It can be useful if models bring some basic accessories such as tights, vests and T-shirts with them – but try not to fall into using 'model's own' pieces too often – it's a lazy solution.

ABOVE — Every single outfit should be photographed on its model and pinned up backstage in the correct running order, as Haizhen Wang did for his SS14 show at London Fashion Week.

ABOVE — White face make-up and a wild hair style bring unity to the models in a Vivienne Westwood show (Photo courtesy of My Beautiful City).

ABOVE — Outrageous hair decoration can entirely change the appearance of a model and might be a simple unifying theme for a show. This approach was used by London-based menswear designer Christopher Shannon for SS14.

LEFT — Retro hairstyles suit the retro styling of designer Henry Holland's feminine collection at London Fashion Week (Photo courtesy of My Beautiful City).

HOW TO CONDUCT YOUR REHEARSALS

One of the main reasons that most 'big-name' catwalk shows comprise merely a parade of models walking up and down the runway is so 'the clothes can speak for themselves', without the distractions of complicated choreography. But it is also because complicated choreography requires lots of rehearsals to do it well. During the hectic schedule of major fashion weeks, such rehearsal time just does not exist. So bear in mind that a complicated show will require plenty of time for practising the moves. It certainly can work, even for a small show, but do not underestimate the commitment in time required from lots of people. If you are working with amateurs you will need to allow for a longer rehearsal time to practise the basic business of how to stand at the head of the catwalk, how long to wait before setting off down the catwalk, how to pose for the photographers, and how to avoid collisions, so making for a smooth production.

LEFT — The models are put through their paces at a rehearsal for a rehearsal at Julien MacDonald's AW14 show in London.

1. Once you have selected your outfits for the show, your models need to try them on with all the correct footwear and accessories. If time allows, alterations should be made to any garments that do not fit perfectly.

2. If you are working with professional dressers it is helpful, but not essential, that they attend the dress rehearsal. They will be able to familiarize themselves with the garments before the show starts. If you are working with amateur dressers it is imperative that they attend the dress rehearsal to get a feel of what is expected of them and to be familiar with each outfit, how it works, how it fastens, how it should look and which accessories go with it. Once you are happy with the outfit, the model should be photographed in the outfit as a reference for the dresser. Each outfit should be given a number to correspond to its appearance and the relevant shoes, bags etc. should also be given the same number.

3. It is recommended that the clothes hangers holding each outfit are secured together with elastic bands and that all the garments are then covered in a polythene bag, as used by dry cleaners, to keep them fresh for the dress rehearsal.

4. The first stage of the rehearsals would be to have the models perform the show just in their ordinary clothes and footwear. This is to get them used to the venue, the music, any choreography, the running order and so on. It gives you the opportunity to time the show (remember – shorter is better than longer) and to check that the layout of the venue works for your show concept.

5. The most important run-through is the technical and dress rehearsal. In this, the models wear the correct outfits to perform the show with the full backing of the lights, music, back projections, voice-overs and any other elements. The models should be in the correct make-up with the hairstyles you want them to wear. By this stage, if your preparation and planning has been correct, the show should need only minor adjustments.

6. The technical and dress rehearsal allows the full production team to be involved, from the controllers of the music and lighting to the dressers, wardrobe mistress and show caller backstage. It may be appropriate to invite to the rehearsal personal friends, work colleagues and other interested parties who will not be coming to the main show.

7. After the dress rehearsals, all the outfits must be recombined and replaced correctly on the rails backstage, ready for the show.

ABOVE — Rehearsals went ahead at Maria Grachvogel's show in London for SS14 even if the hair styles were not quite finished.

ABOVE — Wearing their own clothes, models pace out the runway in a practice for New Zealand-born designer Karen Walker's SSW13 show in New York.

ABOVE RIGHT — Norwegian designer Fam Irvoll likes to use exaggerated hairstyles in her shows.

HOW TO ARRANGE A BACKSTAGE AREA

Backstage is the engine room that drives the show. As it will not be seen by the audience, it does not have to be pretty, but it does have to be efficient, which means, first and foremost, that it has to be large enough to accommodate all the rails of clothes, dressers for each model, hair and make-up team, wardrobe mistress, models and show-production staff. The best backstage area will have everything very close together to minimize the time taken to get the models on stage, off stage, changed and back on again. Professional show organizers insist that getting the backstage area right is one of the main keys to running a successful event.

1. The backstage area should be immediately adjacent to the runway. Having it any distance from the catwalk will only cause undesirable problems.

2. If you are having a raised stage and raised platform out front, of course you will need steps or a ramp up from the backstage area up to the stage. Consider the type of footwear and garments your models will be wearing and make sure the steps are wide enough and not too steep to allow easy access up and down.

3. Hairdressers' and make-up artists' work stations should be placed on the furthermost extremities of the backstage area where they can work out of the way in advance of the show. If circumstances permit, they can be in a separate adjacent area. Once the show is running, it is unlikely that any models will be having significant hair and make-up amendments, so the relevant artists can just stand by the entrance to the catwalk in case any minor tidying is required.

4. Clothes rails should be placed centrally, allowing plenty of space for the models to change. It gets frantic backstage when the show is running and tempers get frayed if people keep accidentally banging into each other. Where possible, all the accessories should be laid out next to each outfit. Jewellery and shoes can be hung in bags on hangers. The dresser can simply remove them in preparation for the next change while the model is on the catwalk.

5. Trestle tables for shared accessories such as hats and shoes should be close enough to the catwalk entrance so that models can collect them en route. Allow room for movement around this – it should not be a pinch point. Ideally, this table will be manned by someone who can keep order, as the clothes are taken up and returned by the models. This ensures that pieces can be smoothly passed from person to person without any panic-stricken scrabbling around.

6. Equipment that might be needed for the dress rehearsal, such as steamers, ironing boards and mirrors, can be removed before the show to maximize the space. Everything should be perfect by the event.

7. Place full-length mirrors near to the entrance of the catwalk.

8 Keep a good space near to the entrance of the catwalk. You will have to allow the models to line up before they go onto the catwalk and for them to come off it without getting in the way of those going on. The show's stylist will stand here to check every model before they go on – they will be maintaining the running order and the caller will be hurrying dressers and models along to ensure that everyone is in place at the right time.

BELOW — Each model will have his or her own rail, with each outfit shown on a numbered photograph. This rail was shot backstage in 2009 at a show by Australian designer Jayson Brundson in Sydney.

ABOVE — A touch of hairspray before hitting the catwalk for the SS14 Sibling show in London.

LEFT — Don't underestimate how many hair stylists you will require, as seen here at the Parkchoonmoo show in New York in February 2012.

ABOVE, RIGHT AND OPPOSITE — Careful planning is needed to make sure that the backstage area for hair and make-up works efficiently, as seen here.

HOW TO ARRANGE THE BACKSTAGE EQUIPMENT

You will need to gather a range of essential equipment backstage to create a working area which functions efficiently and smoothly.

1. Provide clearly named hanging rails. Have ideally one for each model, but definitely no more than two models sharing one rail or you will get a tangled mass of bodies when they are trying to change. The rails also serve as something of a modesty barrier, so the models can change without being on view to everyone (which may be important with amateur models). Professional models of both sexes are used to undressing in front of each other. But if you are using amateurs for a unisex show, you may have to design your backstage area so that the men and women can maintain some modesty.

2. Have plenty of the correct clothes hangers. You should aim to hang every item separately. Layering items can lead to creasing. Don't put heavy coats or dresses on feeble hangers that are designed for shirts. You do not want items dropping to the floor.

3. Plan your backstage area to accommodate trestle tables and chairs. Hairdressers and make-up artists, for example, will need somewhere to lay out their equipment. You will also need a table on which to place shared accessories, such as hats and jewellery, which are being used by more than one model throughout the show. A table will be required for drinks, whether water, soft drinks or alcohol, and perhaps some simple, non-messy food, but this one should be located away from the clothes rails to avoid spills.

4. Backstage, your make-up artists and hairdressers will need good lights to work under. But the main grooming area could be further away from the catwalk than the clothes changing, which has to be immediately adjacent to it.

5. Mirrors will be used by hairdressers and make-up artists while they are working on models. Additionally, you should always have some full-length mirrors to allow models to check that everything is in the right place before they head out onto the catwalk.

6. Remember to bring with you multi-plug extensions and extension cables. Electric sockets may not be conveniently placed, and hairdressers in particular may need to use several different pieces of electrical equipment at once, such as hairdryers and curling tongs.

7. Irons, ironing boards and/or clothes steamers are also essential pieces of equipment. To look pristine, all the clothes must be cleaned and prepared in advance of the dress rehearsal. If they are then hung properly, most will not need ironing again, but having the steamer or iron hot and ready (in a safe position) just in case is a good precaution.

8. Don't forget an emergency repair kit. Buttons can become detached in haste, hems caught and threads pulled, so having needles and threads at the ready will ensure that no time is lost putting things right. The typical emergency repair kit should contain needles and threads of a variety of colours, scissors, pins and safety pins.

9. The clothes on the runway must look pristine, so make sure that you have the equipment on hand for dressers to remove hair, fluff, loose threads and so on. Clothes brushes, lightly damp sponges, fluff removers such as sticky lint rollers, even tweezers, can come in useful. The sticky side of adhesive tape is also good for picking up rogue threads and general fluff.

10. A basic first aid kit is always useful to have on hand. You never know when someone might need some painkillers, antihistamine tablets, antiseptic wipes, lip salve or sticking plasters. Nail scissors and nail files are also useful additions to the kit.

11. Lengths of white silk or cotton can be very useful in protecting the clothes from make-up damage inflicted during quick costume changes. Getting make-up on your own clothes may not be a disaster, but it can cause a bad feeling and leave you with a large post-show dry cleaning bill if it occurs on borrowed merchandise. Borrowed items really ought to be returned in immaculate condition. The main problem occurs when items have to be pulled on and off over the head – if you have a length of white silk you put it over the model's head and face, so that the clothes do not come into contact with the face as they are pulled on and off.

12. If your budget allows, invest in some electric fans. It can get very hot backstage, and models can become overheated as they tear on and off the catwalk and rush to get changed. A fan near the entrance will help cool them down so they feel calm and collected before they return to the runway.

ABOVE — A model is prepared for an Alice Temperley show in London. (Photo courtesy of My Beautiful City).

LEFT — Cosmetics ready for use before the show.

ABOVE — Hair accessories, as seen at the Fred Butler SS13 show, need to be as well organised as all other accessories.

ABOVE — It is always worth investing in the correct hangers for the clothes, as Tata Naka did for their London show for AW14.

ABOVE — Don't attempt to do hair and make-up on models when they are wearing your catwalk clothes; salon gowns are a much safer idea, as Fam Irvoll did for her AW14 show.

HOW TO PUT TOGETHER A GOODY BAG AND PRESS KIT

Having a presentation bag for your most important guest is always a nice gesture, but it is best to do it only if you can get together a memorable goody bag. No goody bag at all is better than a boring or weak one.

1. Make sure that your guests get an opportunity to take away something about you and your company. This could be as simple as a business card or a postcard with your contact details on it. You might add a look book or catalogue and a short background to your company and what you do.

2. As well as the above, the media will need a CD containing high-resolution images of your collection or details of a link to a website from which they can download the images.

3. Even if you don't have a goody bag, you should supply each guest with a credit sheet that lists what they will see in the show, scene by scene. This sheet should also include acknowledgements and thanks, sponsors' details and logos and, most importantly, your contact details, in case attendees want to follow up with you after the event.

4. Fashion shops who stage their own fashion shows or put on one for a charity event find it very useful to include in the goody bag a card that gives an incentive for someone to shop with them. This could be a card giving, say, a 20 per cent discount on purchases within a certain period. Such a device helps drive potential customers to the store; it also allows the shop owner to gauge how much new business or repeat business from customers the catwalk show prompted.

5. Depending on the size of your audience, you may be able to source sample products of items such as fragrance and cosmetics. Large firms may be happy to provide free testers, especially if they have a new product to promote.

6. Drinks suppliers and confectionary companies are also the sort of firms that have large supplies of promotional material to distribute. You may be lucky in getting them to provide you with free samples to distribute at your event.

7. Sourcing very high-quality items for a goody bag is far more difficult than it first appears and, of course, is even more challenging if you need a large number.

8. If you are promoting a local shopping district, some of the retailers may be able to provide interesting small gifts or samples to add to your goody bag.

9. The bag, whether it contains goodies or information about the show, should be a promotional opportunity for the show organizer, so make sure it is of as high a quality as you can afford, that it carries your name and that it reflects you well.

LEFT — Topshop goody bags await the guests at the AW14 show in London.

ABOVE — Presentation is everything: Gift bags from Shiseido await visitors to the Tess Giberson show in New York in September 2013, while (right) programmes and gift boxes are arranged at the Herve Leger by Max Azria SS 2009 event in New York.

LEFT — Staff put out the goody bags at the SS 2006 show for American designer Douglas Hannant in New York.

Louis Vuitton AW 2012, Paris

Luxury fashion brand Louis Vuitton began life as a luggage maker in the 19th century and the golden age of rail travel was recalled in its spectacular show in Paris for AW 2013. A marquee in a courtyard of the Louvre was transformed into a replica of a turn-of-the-20th-century railway station, complete with a full-size steam engine which puffed its way on rails to centre stage. Elegant models descended from a period passenger carriage behind the engine and then paraded around the rectangular catwalk, each accompanied by a diminutive male porter carrying Louis Vuitton's latest bags and cases. This was an astonishing piece of theatre inspired by the heritage of the brand.

AFTER THE SHOW

As is clear from reading this book, organizing an effective fashion show is a huge undertaking. Ideally, the relationship with your audience should not stop after the event has taken place. There is a selection of tasks to be done to ensure that the good impression your show makes is followed with other communications to make your event a long-term success.

1. Make the images or videos from the show available to download, or at least view online. To find out who is viewing or downloading, ensure that everyone has to register on the site first.

2. Very promptly after the event, send the local press and any other relevant media high-resolution images from the show.

3. Send a thank you note to your sponsors and anyone else who helped you. If you made a video of the show, send a copy of it on a DVD or download to the sponsors.

4. At the show, try and collect as much information about your guests as possible, such as name, address, mobile number, email address, how they heard about the event etc. Much of this can be collected beforehand if you manage the invitations online. If yours is a business event, collect business cards from your attendees. This information will be useful to you in the future.

5. For a more informal event, supply everyone with a short form to fill in. Once you have collated some personal details, you will be able to inform the attendees about subsequent shows or other aspects of your business in the future. This type of data capture is very important to enable you to continue to communicate with your target audience.

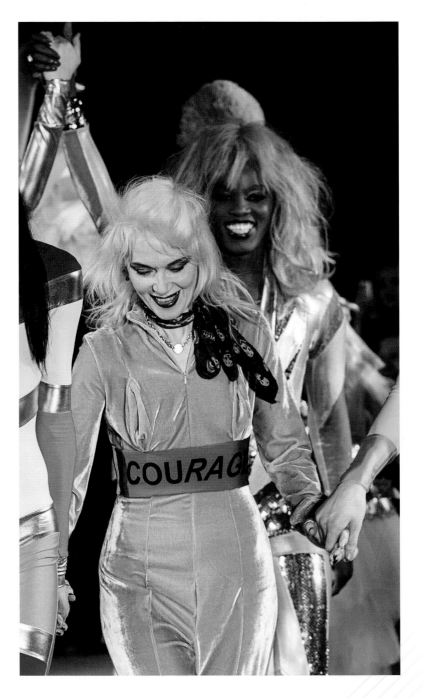

ABOVE — The Tata Naka AW14 show is captured for posterity by photographers and video makers.

LEFT — London-based designer Pam Hogg takes the applause at the end of her AW14 runway show.

GLOSSARY: WHO DOES WHAT?

___

The producer — In some cases, someone wishing to stage a fashion show will hand all the responsibilities over to a show producer. It will be his or her duty to bring the entire project together. An experienced fashion show producer will bring in all the experts required at every stage in the process. The first question they will ask the client is: what is your budget? Everything flows from this consideration.

ABOVE — Lights, cameraman and music on the Apple Mac awaits the arrival of the models at the AW14 presentation by Tata Naka in London.

OPPOSITE — Designer Jamie Wei Huang (right) discusses the finer points of her presentation with producer John Walford.

The stylist — This is the person whose responsibility it is to pull all the clothes and accessories together. Their role can be hugely significant, or quite slight, depending on the kind of show that is being staged. Some stylists will, with the designers, help to create the overall theme and concept. Others will have quite a functional role, such as accessorising pre-selected looks. The stylist can provide a helpful independent overview and play devil's advocate, but their main function is to reflect the image and style their client demands. They should not be afraid to speak out (they are likely to have more experience in staging shows than their client), but their ego must never be allowed to dominate, so they don't dictate a look that either overwhelms or underwhelms the overall purpose of the show.

BELOW AND RIGHT — Celebrated stylist William Gilchrist makes adjustments backstage at an Oliver Spencer show, while (right) Oliver Spencer himself checks the fit of one of his jackets at a rehearsal.

The PR (press relations or public relations person) —

He or she has responsibility for all aspects of publicizing the show. They will draw up a list of guests in consultation with the client, send out invites and deal with responses, and draw up the final list of attendees. They generally oversee the entrance and ensure that people are welcomed to the venue and seated. They will also handle advance publicity and ensure that relevant press and local dignitaries and celebrities are invited.

BELOW — Jamie Wei Huang mixes with her guests at her London show for AW14.

Hair stylist — How your models look has to be part of the overall theme of the show.

Their hairstyles obviously may be a crucial part of that look. Remember that the more complicated a look is, the longer it will take to achieve it. Consider how many models you will want to use – how long will it take to create the look you want? You will need to work closely with a good hair stylist to establish what is feasible. Options can range from very natural looks, highly creative hair styles, wigs or some sort of headwear. Remember the main hair styling should be done before the show, but hair stylists should be backstage during the show just to ensure the effect is perfect when the models embark on the runway.

LEFT — Perfection takes time to create: even short hair can require a lot of preparation.

TOP — The edges of the lips
are accentuated backstage at the
Charlie May show for AW13.

OPPOSITE — Sometimes several
pairs of hands are needed to
produce the final effect. Note that
the eye make-up is as extravagant
as the hair style at Fred Butler's
SS13 show during London
Fashion Week.

Make-up — Most of the points that apply to the hair stylist apply to the make-up team also. Even a touch of make-up will make most people look better in catwalk photographs. Good make-up is possibly even more important if you are using non-professional models. As with the hair, you will need a big enough team of make-up artists to deal with the size of your troupe of models. The main make-up will be applied before the show starts, but someone backstage should do a last-second check before the models hit the catwalk.

The dresser — This person must be reliable and have good attention to detail. The dresser ensures that their model's clothes are all prepared and in the correct order prior to a show. They help to dress and undress the model, ensuring they are in the correct outfit in time to get on the catwalk for their required slot. They keep the models calm before and during the show, tidy everything up at the end and ensure that any wardrobe malfunctions are addressed. Typically, there should be one dresser for each model, but you may need two dressers for complicated outfits such as extravagant evening wear or bridal dresses.

ABOVE — A detailed photo and description of each outfit means nothing is left to chance at a Diesel Black Gold show in Florence in January 2014.

OPPOSITE — Standing room only: last-minute details can be applied just before the show commences.

The model

— It is often said that a model must be able to 'walk'. In fashion jargon, this means that he or she must be able to move fluidly and elegantly and, most importantly, show the clothes to best effect. The model's responsibility is simply to make the clothes look good – and that takes far more skill than one might think. There are many photographic models who are not any good at fashion shows, and vice versa. Similarly, although we tend to think of catwalk models as tall, slim and young, some designers deliberately avoid such stereotypes. In a small-scale show, much fun and effect could be created by including non-conventional models. The most important attribute of an effective model is attitude, and people of all shapes and sizes have that.

RIGHT — A rocker's hairstyle complements the rocker's styling of the shirt.

BELOW — Models are chosen to project the image of a collection.

The caller — The ringmaster backstage is the caller, who has the second-by-second listing of what should be happening and makes sure it happens. He or she is the link between backstage and the front-of-house team. Their most important job is to ensure the right model, in the right outfit, is out on the runway at the right time.

RIGHT — On your marks: the running order for a Diesel Black Gold show in Florence is indicated by tape on the floor.

BELOW — Models in a blue-and-white group wait to hit the runway for Whistles during London Fashion Week. (Photo courtesy of My Beautiful City).

Q&A CREATIVE DIRECTOR

Who are your clients, and what do you do for them?
My Beautiful City has a variety of clients from fashion labels to car brands, mainly based in the luxury sector. We work on product launches, award ceremonies, fashion shows, private parties, film premieres, marketing stunts, permanent installations, packaging redesign and music festivals. Our services include: concept creation, creative design, location sourcing and management, set building and prop hire, casting, logistics, hair, make-up and styling ,video and stills production, photo shoots, experiential digital and multi-media production, talent handling, lighting and sound direction, special effects, choreography, sponsorship and guest list management.

Who are your team members and what are their roles in managing your shows and events?
The team consists of individuals from a wide range of disciplines including production and marketing management, architectural design and 3D animation. Every project is different, each with its own demands so we assign suitable team members to each new brief. There are occasions, such as award ceremonies, when the full agency team is required and others when a single member of the team manages a project solo.

Which show would you say you had the most fun managing? What made it a success?
— Vivienne Westwood (Olympia, Earls Court in 2010)
Terry Hart, our Fashion Director, and I were advised by the British Fashion Council not to hold the show at Olympia due to its distance from central London. We went ahead as the space had never been used for a fashion show before and it gave us scope to be adventurous with the creative. To tie in with the collection's African theme we worked with United Visual Artists to create a striking visual of the sun which gradually set over the course of the show. My fear in the week running up to the show was that no one would turn up, but when the time came you literally couldn't move. We had over 1,000 people try to get in!
— Rag and Bone (Sloane Square in 2012)
My Beautiful City were the first people to propose putting a marquee up on Sloane Square and holding a fashion show there. We had to persuade the council and jump through a lot of red tape. To finally get approval and see the show go ahead on the square was hugely rewarding.

Name three of the most important factors to consider when putting on a fashion show.
— Location: Often this is the first thing we have to consider and is also the element that influences the creative.
— Creative: This is what My Beautiful City is all about. We pride ourselves on outstanding and original creative concepts.
— Budget: This should never be used to limit ideas but obviously plays a crucial part in planning.

There are so many stages to putting on a successful show: building a concept, planning a budget, recruiting a team… where would you say is the best place to begin?
The building of a strong team behind you is absolutely crucial. Shows can be stressful at the best of times and having a network of people who are experts in their fields and who can keep a cool head at all times is key. As an agency, we like to push creative boundaries and the only reason we continue to be able to do this is that we are all extremely passionate about what we do and when required we pull together to support each other.

**Robin Scott Lawson
Creative Director and Founder, My Beautiful City**

ABOVE — Behind the scenes at the Julien McDonald AW14 Show.
Produced by My Beautiful City.

ACKNOWLEDGEMENTS

The observations made in this book are based on my experience of more than 34 years of attending fashion events and writing about fashion. I would like to thank, in particular, certain specialists who helped me clarify my thoughts: Barbara Mason of the London-based Production Team and Andy Shorten of Different Day in Folkestone. I was assisted by the experiences shared by retailing friends who have staged many events for their own shops over the years: Annie Furbank of Anne Furbank in Buckden, St Neots, Cambridgeshire; and Hilary Cookson of Maureen Cookson in Whalley, Lancashire. Thanks also to David Carter-Johnson of creative agency My Beautiful City for connecting the publisher with the company's picture archive. I am grateful for the efforts of photographer Andy Barnham to provide us with some fine visuals. My daughter Florence Eastoe proved to be very reliable as a proof reader. Finally, as always, I need to thank my wife Jane Eastoe for her unstinting support and thoughtful insights based on her own many years as a fashion writer.

RIGHT — The striking designs of Ashish Gupta highlighted on the London Fashion Week catwalk for AW14.

OPPOSITE — Savile Row-based Richard James used a BMW showroom on Park Lane as the venue for his catwalk show during London Collections: Men for SS14 (Photo courtesy of My Beautiful City).